THE
CORRIDORS
OF
A
CERTAIN
LIFE

All glory and honor be unto my God

My prayer to God
during a very difficult time:
"God please give me something to do
with my mind and hands"
His answer:
"Write"

Thank Yous:

To Pastors Robert and Lorinda Dailey
For building a strong foundation

To Cynthia Snow
Who helped bring forth the revelation
by writing on my facebook page
"You're writing"

To my sister Akilah Nayo
Who was my inspiration
and encouragement
while writing this book

To my daughters and my grandson
Marqueta, Myesha and A.J.
For their contributions to this book

This book is dedicated to my mother:

Melvaline Anna Jean Oliver
1/22/1935 – 10/16/2009

'I AM MY MOTHER'S DAUGHTER'

Mother you taught me that anything
is possible when you apply yourself.
You instilled in me
"dare to believe" and achieve.
You always continued to
put one foot in front of the other
despite the circumstances.

Your life has been a vivid example of
strength, faith, fortitude and triumph.
Through the ups and the downs,
the ins and the outs *love* prevailed.

And what feels like an end to me,
is really just a beginning
for the both of us.

May my life be a reflection of you!

FOREWORD

I THANK OUR LORD AND SAVIOR JESUS CHRIST for giving Ms. Marcia (from our St. Louis Dream Center days) the boldness to speak and share her story of pain, joy, and victories. She has unselfishly poured out her heart in *The Corridors of a Certain Life*. She has worked tirelessly to ensure the lives of women are changed by the power of God. And she writes!! I have been blessed to know Marcia Oliver during the years, as she wept, questioned, laughed, danced, and ran from and through the corridors of her life. As you read *The Corridors of a Certain Life* you will find that integrity, transparency, and the love of God are the overwhelming themes in this touching-of-the-heart book. She explains the season of her life as hallways. Seasons, like corridors, may be lengthy or they may end abruptly. The reader will soon learn that sometimes we do not have the option to pick our seasons or our corridors. We may innocently or knowingly wander through the corridors and fail to appreciate that in them, God has destiny and purpose for our lives. Yet, in other corridors we are keenly aware of our place in God, as we celebrate each day in faith, knowing our God will direct our footsteps. *The Corridors of a Certain Life* will give direction and inspire the reader who is struggling with the uncertainties and the unfairness of life. The reader is encouraged by knowing that our Faithful God remains in control of our lives.

If we are honest, we may recognize a glimpse of ourselves in *The Corridors of a Certain Life* as we walk though each corridor reflecting and remembering a time when we were faced with a similar situation. One may simply sit in a hallway and smile as Marcia shares her God-given insight on grace and mercy. Another may weep, as he discovers how to apply Psalm 136 as his personal testimony. Men and women alike will laugh out loud as they learn how to toss a hot potato to the Lord or learn to appreciate the "TH" sound.

There is a certainty; we will go through different corridors within our lifetime. We can rest assured that God desires the best of us and sees the best in us. He sees us covered with the blood of Jesus. God sees us as victorious and walking through each corridor in spirited triumph.

It was an honor to be asked to write the foreword to *The Corridors of a Certain Life.* As you read to the end of this book, I am praying that our God will speak to your heart as He has spoken to mine and reassure you that no season is too difficult to get through, when we allow Jesus to lead us through every corridor of our life.

~ Cynthia Matthews Snow

THE CORRIDORS

HALLWAY
I

Hey God, It's Me, Marcia

ANOTHER SLEEPLESS NIGHT

I toss and I turn
I fall in and out of sleep
I need rest so off to the tub I go

I emerge myself in a tub of warm water
My body begins to relax
I feel calmness and peace

And You are there
If I can hear a word from You
Then I'll know what to do
So, I listen

I grab a couple of hours of sleep
I wake up
And realize
I have to leave my haven
And face the world again

Hurry Tomorrow

"Hurry tomorrow,
tomorrow I need you now!"

What is the urgency in tomorrow?

The urgency is
to get beyond this
VERY PRESENT MOMENT!

This moment
that is so overbearing
so overwhelming
and so endless.

This moment
that is so dark
so debilitating
and so frightening.

Tomorrow
is my hope,
my promise
and my confirmation

That this moment too shall pass.

Joy comes in the morning!!!!!

Me

I am a Woman of God
A daughter of the Most High
I am an heir to righteousness

I am sociable
But I also walk around
In my head
90% of the time
Which means you can be standing
Right in front of my face
And I may not see you

I don't waste energy disliking people
I don't try to figure out whether
Or not people like me
We are all trying to make it through
This thing called "life"

I know that God places people
In my life for a reason
Even if it's only for a season
I have rarely met anyone whom
I did not learn something from

My Shout
(Inspired by Kenneth W. Jones, Sr)

Shout to the Lord!!!

Someone once told me
I needed to shout.

But how?
What would I shout?
Where is my shout?
WHY CAN'T I SHOUT?

My shout is buried deep inside.

Maybe I can't shout
Because I'm afraid
Of the eruption that may occur.

Or maybe

I can't shout
Due to the fear
Of the walls crumbling down.
And me,
being totally exposed.

Psalm 51

Renew in me a right spirit

I want to be of a humble spirit
And a contrite heart

I want to hang out with God

Psalm 136
(*made personal*)

O give thanks unto the Lord;
For He is good;
For His mercy endureth forever.

O give thanks unto the God of gods;
For His mercy endureth forever.

O give thanks to the Lord of lords;
For His mercy endureth forever.

To Him who alone doeth great wonders;
For His mercy endureth forever.

To Him that by wisdom made the heavens;
For His mercy endureth forever.

To Him that stretched out the earth
Above the waters;
For His mercy endureth forever.

To Him that made great lights;
For His mercy endureth forever.

The sun to rule by day;
The moon and stars to rule by night;
For His mercy endureth forever.

To Him that delivered me
From depression;
And brought me out of darkness;
For His mercy endureth forever.

With a strong hand,
And with a stretched out arm;
For His mercy endureth forever.

To Him that gives me wisdom;
And allows me to shine;
For His mercy endureth forever.

Who shields me
Against the fiery weapons;
For His mercy endureth forever.

To Him who never leaves me
Nor forsakes me;
For His mercy endureth forever.

To Him who held me
Through my mother's death;
And escorts me through
Every difficult situation;
For His mercy endureth forever.

To Him that has moved me onward;
For His mercy endureth forever.

From Los Angeles to St. Louis;
For His mercy endureth forever.

From St. Louis to Baton Rouge;
For His mercy endureth forever.

From Baton Rouge to Indianapolis
and back again;
For His mercy endureth forever.

Who remembered me
In my low estate;
For His mercy endureth forever.

And hath redeemed me
From my enemies;
For His mercy endureth forever.

Who awakens me and teaches me;
For His mercy endureth forever.

O give thanks unto the God of heaven;
For His mercy endureth forever.

PURPOSE

God, what is my purpose?

Please direct my path
Towards the purpose
For which I was called.

I will acknowledge You in all my ways.
I will seek You all of my days.

My hope and my trust
Are in You.

Everything You have created
Has its perfect place.

The birds of the air.
Lions... tigers... monkeys and even bears.
The fish in the deep blue sea.

All know and live in their perfect space.

Lord please place me!
Order my steps,
Show me Your plan.

You chose to place me in this race.
Please let me see Your face!

I will seek You in the morning.
I will seek You in the noon day.
I will praise and magnify Your name.

I will continue to proclaim
That You are
"The great I am, that I am"

I will chase after You
All the days of my life.

I don't want stuff
Or even the acceptance of man.

All I really want
Is to be in Your perfect plan.

Lord what is my purpose?

Reflections

In my bed on 99th street...
Praying desperately to a God
I knew nothing about

In the kitchen at Grandma Cook's house
After professing
That I didn't believe in God...
Grandma Cook saying,
"Marcia's gonna be alright"

Sitting on the edge of my bathtub
After gall bladder surgery...
Holy Spirit spoke these words to me:
"The enemy comes
to steal, kill and destroy
(emphasis on kill)
Watch Mrs. Dailey
she has something to impart to you"

Sister Nena speaking life to me
At Dr. Barconey's office...
"You shall live and not die..."

Late in the midnight hour
In my bedroom...
"Lord my heart's desire is to do Your will"

Being slain in the Holy Spirit...
Even though this time
I was determined not to go down.

In my Aunt Peggy's basement
In St. Louis...
"Lord if You send me I'll go"

On my knees at one of the Ark of God's
Visions Conference...
saying *"God use me, I surrender all to You"*

Pacing the living room floor (music blasting):
*"Lord what am I here for,
what is it You would have me to do?"*

Sitting at my desk
At Caring to Love Ministries saying...
*Satan you should have killed me
while you had the chance*

When I reflect back
And look at where I am at this very moment
All I can say is
God hears and He answers!!!!

I reflect on so many things
I have yet to understand.
But I know
It's all a part of God's plan
Past, present and future.

HALLWAY

II

I see.....People

Because of You Guys

"I am so happy to be amongst the living"
Those are the words
To a Yolanda Adams song.
Those words are resounding
Throughout my mind right now.
There was a time in my life
When I thought life was just too hard
And I did not want to be amongst the living.

During my most desperate moments
God used just plain old folks
To help me through;
Often times and even today,
I don't think they know what an important role
They played in my life.

I just want to list these people by name:

Debra Temple,
who accepts and loves me as I am
(my bff),

Pastor Robert and Lorinda Dailey
(my spiritual mother and father),

Grandma Cook
(who I know prayed me through),

Candi
(my stepmom),

Marqueta and Myesha
(my daughters),

Kim, Mandisa and Akilah
(my sisters),

Oluchi
(my nephew),

Stevie Phillips, Maursid Gaston, Chubie Egbuho,
Odee Egbuho, David Dailey, Renee Stevenson,
Nena Sanders, Debbie Kelley,

Lois Amantine
(for always speaking the truth to me in love),

Pat Ortiz, Sherry Meadows, Gloria Amantine,
Tony James, Dennise Dailey, Minta Collins,

Carlos Batchelor
*(he loved me enough not to come to my pity
parties),*

Virginia Temple, Cynthia Snow, Alliece Cole,
Tony Gilmore, Pastor Aubrey,
Pastor Jeff and Jaime Allensworth,

Taneka Ohmer
(for standing by my side),

Adam and Kim Braud, Donna Kelley,
Aunt Peggy, Aunt Dorothy,

Cherry, Evonne, Terri, Derrick, Jimmy Mack,
Rachel and Lynne
(My cousins)

Don and Dorothy Wallis
(for unconditional love),

Rebecca Bibbins
(who opened her home to me),

Rose Willis, Marisa King, Ella Sue Evan,
Rose Polk, Pastor Albert and Adriane White

Elizabeth Washington
(who made me laugh
when I thought I never would again),

and
My mom Melvaline Oliver

God used all these people
At different points and times in my life,
When I truly thought
I could not go on another day.

I thank all of you for allowing God to use you.

And if you didn't know
That you had ever been used by God,
Now you know!

"Big Donna"

1957 – 2007

I Remember...
82nd and Normandie
Playing with barbie dolls
at the top of the stairs and
Making soap in the front yard

I Remember...
LaSalle Elementary School (87th Street School)
Getting my hair done and
Donna popping me with that comb

I Remember...
Listening to music
Thinking, *"Dang that girl can dance"*
Horace Mann Junior High School
(feeling protected because of who Donna was)

I Remember...
Hanging out at Denny's
The Holidays
The kids' birthday parties

I Remember...
Donna hanging at the back
of the Ark of God Ministries
In case she had to make a quick getaway

I Remember...
Sitting in the bedroom
Sometimes the living room
Philosophizing about life
or
On the porch having a smoke

Her smile lit up the entire room
And warmed the hearts of others

I thank God for my cousin
"Big Donna"

She watched out for me
She loved me
She advised me
She hung out with me
She rebuked me
She taught me
She corrected me

"Thank you Donna"

For helping me become
The woman that I am

Grannilocks

1935 - 2009

My Mother
The biggest part of me!

"Mommy"
You raised me
You fed me
You protected me
You sheltered me
You corrected me
You chastised me
But most of all
YOU LOVED ME

"Ma"
You fought for me
You fought with me
Never once did you fight against me
You would not give up on me
And you would not allow me
To give up on myself
YOU LOVED ME

"Mother"
You encouraged me
You lifted me up
You strengthened me
You shared your wisdom
You always had my back
You let me see you
YOU LOVED ME

"Grannilocks"
3RD and 4TH generation
You continued
To encourage
To affirm
To lead
To direct
To teach
To share wisdom
To uplift
To build
as
YOU CONTINUED TO LOVE

And it is that Love
That will continue
To motivate us
Through this journey called "Life"

I miss you so much
But your legacy ***shall*** live on

So, rest in peace
"Melvaline Anna Jean Bobo"

Knowing that through your life
You have taught us
To love
To live
To share
and
To give

You have given us
Strength
Wisdom
Compassion
and
Faith

We are going to be alright
Because it is your legacy we carry!!!!

Hey Sista Girl

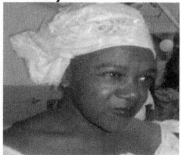

To: *Debbie Temple*
(My BFF)

Hey Sista Girl!

You've been
My friend
My confidant
My spiritual sister

You always believed in me
"You can do anything you put your mind to"
"You are so smart"
You believed in me
When I didn't/couldn't believe in myself

I remember when we first met
I remember thinking to myself
Who is this girl
All up in my space
Not to mention my face

We have been through a lot
From Africa to Guyana
From Los Angeles to St. Louis

We have been separated
And reunited
You have stood by me
Through all my insanity
And loved me anyway

Remember this
"I gotta go pray for Magic"
And what did you say and do
"Okay let's go!"
And off we headed to the Forum

Your friendship means
The world to me
Time and distance
Has not been able to break the bond

And I just wanna say
I love you, sista girl!

In Remembrance of Marc
(My Big Brother)

1957 – 1980
(died in a parachuting drill in Okinawa, Japan)

He was my big brother
He was like SUPERMAN to me
I thought he was all-knowing

Then I found out
He was only human

And then he was gone

I wish I had gotten to know him for real

In Remembrance of Oluchi
(My Nephew)

1982 - 2003

Lou Pooh
I miss you SO much
But I thank you
For keeping an eye out

When I think of you
I think of a children's rhyme
*Oluchi was here
But now he's gone
He left his art
to carry on...*
I think about your graffiti
Your mark on the world

There was a premonitory wisdom
That you possessed
"You are about to have that pain"

There was a beautiful innocence
That you possessed
*"I'm the baby
gotta love me!"*

I remember
THE LIGHT...

I guess you found it!

"Little Donna"
B.K.A.
Akilah Nayo Oliver

1961 - 2011

My little sister
My mind is flooded
With memories of you
Excerpts from our life
Are constantly
Being played
In my mind
All day
Everyday

It appears
Anything and everything
Triggers a memory
My heart is missing you
But I am so very proud of you

Childhood Flash
I remember how proud you made me feel
When you announced at the dinner table
"My big sister takes good care of me"
Frankie was picking on you
That day at assembly
And I told her to leave you alone

Teen Years Flash
Sitting at the kitchen table reading poems
By Sonia Sanchez, Amiri Baraka,
Nikki Gionvanni, Mari Evans,
Langston Hughes,
"I Too Sing America"
"Mother to Son"

The pride I felt
Seeing that you had obtained
A place amongst those
We so admired as youngsters
"A Toast in the House of Friends"
"Tales of Taliba"

Early Womanhood Flash
Jefferson Townhomes, hanging out
Playing Jeopardy
Playing Scrabble with Luchi and Queta
And then putting them to bed
So we could play for real

So proud
My little sister was a school teacher

Womanhood Flash

The pain in your eyes
Losing your only son
"A Band of Angels Coming Forth"
You holding on to Luchi's shoes
As I still held on to Marc's boots

Realizing though we were very different
We were also very much alike
Agreeing to disagree
And yet
continuing to love and respect one another

Proud to know through your pain
You reached out to others
To help them
Through their pain

Donna,
I remember
People sometimes thought you were shy
But I knew
You were observing and taking everything in
"still waters run deep"
*"better to be thought a fool
than to speak and remove all doubt"*

Yep, though you are gone from this earth
One thing I know
You will always live on in my heart

You are a part of me
And I love you dearly
And not even death can take that!

Remember when we use to recite
"O Death Where is Your Sting"
By Charles Lawrence Dunbar

Well it's now a reality for me.

"Little Donna"
You sure did make a big mark
On this world!

Motherhood

A Mother's Eyes see...
The Good
The Beauty
The Potential

A Mother's Heart feels...
The Pain
The Hurt *(hurt my child and you hurt me)*
The Joy
The Pride
The Hope

A Mother's Arms and Hands...
Reach out
Uphold
Cradle
Hug

A Mother's Words...
Encourage
Comfort
Reassure

A Mother's Instinct is to...
Love
Protect
Nurture

A Mother's Wisdom is to...
Let Go and Let God!!

My Mentor

She challenged me
She upheld me
She pushed me

She infuriated me
She brought out the fight in me
She challenged me

She caused me pain
She penetrated walls
She infuriated me

She stretched me
She caused me to grow

Thank You!

Ode to Dorothy Wallis

A baby cried out to God
"I want to live"
A Young woman prayed
"Lord, I want my baby"

Satan whispered a lie
"It's only a blob"

Another baby cried out
"I want to live"
Another young woman said
"I just don't think I can"

Satan whispers another lie
"This is going to ruin your life"

More babies cried
"Lord, I want to live"

Then He asked
"Dorothy will you go?"
And she said
"Yes, Lord"

OVER 55,000 BABIES SAVED!

Pastor Robert Dailey

1938 – 2010

God placed a man in my life
Not just any man
But a good man

He dispelled the myth that
"A man ain't good for nothing"

He was patient with me
He was kind
And he called me "sweetheart"

God placed a good man in my life
A man who I could call on
Anytime, anywhere
A man who taught me the word of God

He was my neighbor
He was my teacher
He was my spiritual father

He showed me how a "real man"
Provides for and takes care of his family

He showed how a "pastor"
Watches over his flock

He showed me God in the form of a man
In the way he lived
In the way he spoke
In the way he loved

Yes
God placed a good man in my life!

TITUS 2

Can you not see that young woman
Standing before you,
Trying her best to get your attention?

Are you unable to look past her attitude
And facial expressions
To see her heart?

Do you not realize
She is acting out
To illicit a response from you?

She watches you
She admires you
She desires to learn from you.

Do you really not know why
She has been placed in your path?

Or
Are you just too afraid to accept
The responsibility
Of having someone
Look to you
For some of life's answers?

Are you afraid to open your heart?

HALLWAY

III

To God be the Glory

A Grandmother's Prayer

Dear Heavenly Father

I lift my grandchildren to You
Keep them and protect them
Mold them into the man and woman
You would have them to be

Lord, You choose their friends
Place the correct teachers in their lives
Give them knowledge to excel
Grant them favor with
God and man at all times

Speak to their hearts
I pray they recognize Your voice
May they follow You all the days of their lives

Be their comforter
Be their answer
Meet their needs
Bless and direct their paths

Give their parents wisdom
And the vision for their children's life
Bless and instruct their parents

Thank you Lord,
For never leaving them or forsaking them
Thank you,
For Your perfect plan in their lives

Deja Vu

I've been in this place before
I thought I'd never be here again
How did I get here?

I let my circumstances direct me
Took my eyes off You
Drifted Away
Slowly but surely

Forgot who I am
Forgot who my Father is
Forgot His Promises to me
Allowed myself to be deceived

Everything became so cloudy
I couldn't see
But then I remembered
And I cried out Your Name
JESUS!!!!

The path became clear again
I was able to see
And there You were
In this place once again
To lead me out once again

Thank You, Lord!

Fill Her Up...

Fill her up...

Fill her mouth
her eyes
her ears

Fill her up...

Fill her mind
her soul
her body
her heart

Thank you Lord for
Filling me up

Grace and Mercy

The **other day**
I was thinking how grateful I am
for
God's Grace and Mercy

Thinking had it not been
for
His Grace and Mercy
Where might I be

Thankful for my salvation

But somewhere in my mind
I was thinking that Grace and Mercy
Were part of the package of salvation.

Then I realized
That Grace and Mercy
Were a prerequisite for my salvation

Had God's Grace and Mercy
not kept me
Before I ever knew who He was
I wouldn't even be here today
To talk about
His Grace and Mercy.

Hallelujah,
Thank you for Your Grace and Your Mercy.

Name Above All Names

Yet another morning I awaken.

Before I can even open my eyes
I am greeted with the sickness,
The nausea, the sweats, the dizziness,
The headache, the weakness
And all the side effects of the medicine.
The sickness makes me sad.

As I become cognizant
I began to pray healing over my body.
Calling my body, mind and soul
Into submission.

I plead the blood of Jesus.
Knowing all names must bow
To the name of Jesus.

Diabetes must bow,
High Blood Pressure must bow,
High Cholesterol must bow,
All names must bow!

I begin to praise and bless
My God and Lord:

Bless the Lord oh my soul
And all that is within me
Bless His Holy name.
Bless the Lord oh my soul
And forget not all His benefits.
Who forgiveth all thine iniquities.
Who healeth all thy diseases.
Who redeemeth thy life from destruction...

Having had my strength renewed.
I now make a conscious decision
To get up out of my bed
And place one foot in front of the other.

Thanking and praising God the whole time!

Yes, I made the conscious decision,
But no doubt about it
I know I am being carried.

Thank you Jesus!

I will continue to press toward the mark.
Knowing I can do all things
Through Christ who strengthens me.

Oh, Thank Heaven

I am so grateful to be amongst the living

I have spent the last several years
Stepping out in faith
(Sometimes being pushed out)

God has and is doing
Such awesome things in my life
He has given me an assignment
He is guiding and instructing me through it
There are times when I wonder
If I can really fulfill this assignment

But I stand on His word
All my faith and hope
Is in the Lord

I once declared
"This is the best of times
And this is the worst of times"

The best of times
Because it is totally awesome
To be in God's will

The *worst* of times
Because sometimes the obstacles
Appear to be so enormous

Thank God the battle is not mine!!!!!!!!!!!!!

Proverbs 3:5

Let us trust in the lord

Trust He has our back
Trust He is directing our path
Trust He will give us favor
Trust He has the perfect plan for our lives

Trust as we give Him all the praise, all the glory
and all the honor

TRUST

Spiritual Warfare

Spiritual warfare is not
Some vague, nonspecific war
It is an ongoing war
That encompasses many battles
Each time you go into battle
You must know your enemy

And the enemy is not the same
in each battle
So put on your full armor
But know your enemy

The sword of truth is our weapon
(The word of God)
But you must know
Which sword to use in which battle

"The word" of God is not just one word
And the only way you know which sword to use
Is to know which enemy you are battling

You don't use a clove of garlic
To fight a werewolf
You don't shoot a vampire
With a silver bullet.

The Holy Spirit will reveal
What spirit you are in battle with
And even better
He will tell you
what weapon you need for the battle

In between battles
There will be a time of rest
That is a time for
Reflecting and rebuilding

Your rest time is not just sleep time
It is quiet time to hear from the Lord
To receive instructions
And to prepare for the next battle

What an awesome God we serve!!!!!!!!!!!!!!!!

Take No Offense

JESUS WILL TAKE ALL OF OUR BURDENS

OFFENSE IS JUST ANOTHER BURDEN

WHEN YOU GET OFFENDED
(REAL OR IMAGINED)
TREAT IT LIKE A HOT POTATO
AND TOSS IT TO THE LORD

What an Awesome God We Serve

Just take a moment
Stop and look around you;
The sky, the trees, the people!

Have you ever seen a flower bud open?
Have you ever smelled a rose?

Have you ever seen a palm tree
Bend almost to the breaking point
And then rise again?

Have you ever planted a seed
And then seen it break through the ground?

Have you ever watched Wild Kingdom
And marveled at the lifestyles of the animals?
Have you ever seen a dog have pups
And then care for her litter?

Have you ever considered
The flow of human blood
Throughout the body?
In from the veins and out via the arteries
(what a mind blowing process,
amazing how the heart works)
Also amazing is
How a woman's body not only can birth life,
But can also sustain life!

All of these are God's PLANNED creations!
There is a reason
A rose smells the way it does.
There is a reason
Bears hibernate in the winter.
There is a reason and a purpose
For every organ in the human body.
It's all a part of God's Perfect Plan.

Now the part that really excites me is...
To think that this MASTER PLANNER
Has a perfect plan for my life.

The plan started before my conception in my
mother's womb
And is a completed work!

I don't just happen to be here!

There is a reason and a purpose for
Everything that has been,
Everything that is
And everything that is to come in my life!

LET EVERYTHING THAT HAS BREATH
PRAISE THE LORD
HALLELUJAH!!!!!!!!!!!!!!!!!!!

HALLWAY
IV

Thoughts

As a Man Thinketh
Honesty
I Never Realized
Just Thinking Out Loud (Aloud)
Life's Journey
Love Ties
One in Christ
Perfect Peace
Pressure
The Grass is Greener on the Other Side
The Perfect Hiding Place

As a Man Thinketh

I am thinking something that I don't want to say.
As a man thinketh in his heart so he is!
The thoughts I am fighting against right now
Are not in my heart, they are in my mind.
I know that the mind is the battlefield.
I realize this is spiritual warfare.

Lord I plead the blood over my mind.
I have the mind of Christ.
I will walk by faith and not by sight
I will continue to renew my mind daily.

His sheep knows His voice
And the voice of a stranger (deceiver)
They will not follow;
They will flee from it!
He calls his own sheep by name
And He leads them out.

Thank you Jesus!!!!!!!!!!!

Honesty
(dedicated to Tony Richardson)

I prefer HONESTY
even if it hurts

Please deal with me honestly
or don't deal with me at all

Excuses for not being honest are
"I knew you were going through a rough time"
"I didn't want to hurt your feelings"
"I didn't feel it was my place to tell you that"

MALARKY!!!!!!!!!!!!!!

When I say honesty
I mean wrapped in love
Not self-serving, hateful or vindictive

Long, long, long time ago
Someone once told me
"Sometimes people need
to get their feelings hurt"
At the time I thought it was mean

I now concur...

I Never Realized...

When I was in High School
My best friend Cathy's brother died.
I saw her sadness,
I thought I understood her hurt.
I never realized...

Two years after High School
My brother died.
I then realized
That I'd had no idea of Cathy's pain.

The bible says
The older women should
Teach the younger women.
I remember when Gloria was telling me about
The changes our body goes through.
I was not interested.

I remember thinking it was funny
Seeing my mom and my friend Anella
Fanning and breaking out into sweats
Out of nowhere.
Always asking
"Aren't you guys hot?"
I never realized...

Then it happened to me
Suddenly being totally overcome
With a heat from within
Freezing everyone in the house and office
Because "I'm hot."

Tossing and turning all night
Covers on, covers off.
Not so funny now.

I remember when
My Aunt Minta died.
I felt devastated, the tears would just flow.
Thinking my pain was
The same pain my cousins were feeling
I never realized...

October 2009
My mom died.
I never knew that a "broken heart"
Could cause actual pain.
I never imagined that after my mom died
I would have to constantly
Remind myself she was actually dead.
I never knew that I would pick up the phone
To call her
And then remember...

So unaware of the pain that would occur
On a constant basis.
The tears that would flow
With or without permission
I never imagined that a pain could last for so long

I NEVER REALIZED...

Just Thinking Out Loud (Aloud)
(memories of Kim Harris and Adrian Taylor)

...Ace Coon Boon
or was it Ace Boon Coon.
I guess that is something like
my dawg, my homie, my nigga
or my BFF.

...And can you really have
more than one best friend?
Doesn't the word "best"
indicate above all the rest?

I guess you could have a different best friend
at a different time
and for a different reason,
But then that would make the present best friend
a former best friend
or just a friend.

...I remember a conversation from long ago
"What's your name?"
"My name is Keif"
"You mean to tell me
your mother named you Keif?"
"Yes"
"Spell it"
"K-e-i-t-h"
"Boy, your name is KEITH!"

Come on people, the combination of "th"
does not make the "f" sound.

...But you know, the funny thing is,

when Keif and me went to da restrunt
da otha day
There was no lack of communication,
because Keif is my dawg
my Ace Coon Boon!

Okay, I'm going on brain overload!
Isn't it sad I could
overload my brain with such trifling stuff?
Or is it really just an escape?

Check it out,
I just went full circle!!!

Life's Journey
(inspired by Minister Adraine White)

As we walk down this road called "Life,"
we must continuously move forward toward
our destination.
As we arrive upon our destination,
new destinations arise.

My destinations are mapped by God,
therefore, I must keep my sights on Him
to arrive at my destination.
I can't focus on the destination
because sometimes I don't even know
what or where the destination is.

God has provided me with a "Tour Guide"
through life's journey.
But what do you do when you are on the road
and can no longer see the Tour Guide?
That can be very dangerous and very scary,
especially when you are on a course
you are unfamiliar with.
If you turn in the wrong direction
you could end up in a bad place,
or it just might be a very long, round-about way
to arriving at your destiny
(it may be a road with a lot more
trials and tribulations).

When I can no longer see my Tour Guide
it's time to take action.

I once heard an analogy
spoken by Minister Adraine White
that put it all in focus for me:
It's like when you are looking at TV
and something gets between you and the view,
you basically have two options:
move the obstacle or reposition yourself.
Pretty simple!

Sometimes God tells us
just to reposition ourselves,

But you know how that goes:
"Get out the way,"
"Mom, tell her to get out the way!"
Popping her upside the head
and then having to engage in a fight.

When in actuality, all you had to do
was scoot over a little
and the TV was in complete view again.

Amazing how simple life's answers can be.

Love Ties

There is nothing that can separate
"love ties"
Not distance
Not lifestyles
Not time
Not even death

So, though I say farewell for now
I look forward to the day
That we are reunited

One in Christ

We have so many similarities

Yet so different

I'm trying not to get stuck
On the differences

It just seems
Sometimes the differences outweigh
The similarities

Perfect Peace

Death where is your sting?
Grave where is your victory?

To be absent from the body
Is to present with God.

All things work together for good
For those who love God
And are called according to His purpose.

Pressure

Pressure is not necessarily a bad thing
It can in fact be a good thing

Think about it...
Pressure can catapult you to another place

The Grass is Greener on the Other Side

The grass on the other side is greener
Because it is being tended to.
The owner is making sure it gets
Watered, weeded, mowed, etc.

And then you want to go to the other side
Because the grass is greener.
You get there and sit, doing nothing.
You sit for so long
The grass beneath you
Starts to wither and turn brown.

Now, thanks to you,
The owner of the greener grass
has to work harder.
Moving you around
Trying to make you productive also.
Then replenishing what you have caused to die.

So instead of destroying someone else's hard work,
Observe what the owner has done to flourish.
And if you go to the other side,
Then see what you can do
To help him flourish further.

Then apply what you have learned
to your own grass!

The Perfect Hiding Place

I have found the perfect hiding place
A place I can go
And no one can see my face
When I'm there I can say whatever I want
And no one can look into my soul
As I speak

I don't have to worry about
Someone seeing me cry
Or seeing the hurt I feel

"All ye, all ye come free"

But I won't come out of my hiding place
You will have to try to find me
If you can

I will continue to hide right here
Behind my written words

HALLWAY V

How I Got Ova'

Conversation with God
God's Peace
He Is My Safe Place
HOPE
Life's Battles
My Inalienable Rights
Out There
Over or Under
Rest Time
Speak to My Heart Lord
Survivor
Truth or Fact?
Wrestling with God
Yea Though I Walk Through the Valley
of the Shadow of Death

Conversation with God

Me: Lord I need healing, please heal my body.

God: With my stripes you are healed.

Me: Thank you Lord, I receive it.

God: Then walk in it.

Me: I will.

I immediately take my eyes off me
and begin to pray for others.

God's Peace

When my mom died
I wondered if the pain and sadness
Would ever end

Almost 2 years later
My sister died and
I was convinced it wouldn't

5 years later
Thank you Lord for peace
You took me day by day
Moment by moment
You never left me
Or forsook me

You filled this broken heart
With your love and peace

The peace of God
Passes all understanding

He Is My Safe Place

I needed a safe place
I could not bear the thought of the hurt
I wanted to be set free
But, I needed a safe place

And lo and behold!
He was and is my safe place

HOPE

HOPE will get you to the other side of this,
no room or time for despair
HOPE will take you there.

Life's Battles

There's always going to be a battle in life.

I once liken my life
to that of a boxer.
Here I was in this ring
constantly getting the heck beaten out of me.

When the bell would ring
I would drag myself back to my corner.
Unfortunately, all I had in my corner was
self-hatred, pity, anger
and all the cares and injustices of the world.

The bell would ring again.
And I would go back into the ring
for more beatings.
Eventually I laid there
and just waited for the 10 count.
10, 9, 8, 7, 6, 5, 4...

But with whatever little was left in me
I got up and I staggered
back to my corner.

There in my corner were some new faces.
SALVATION and HOPE!!

This time when the bell rang
I returned to the ring
with a little more strength.

Though I lost another round,
next time I returned to my corner
not only were there more new faces
JOY, FAITH and LOVE,
but several of the old faces were gone!

Though the fight is not over.
I get stronger with each round.
And each time I retreat to my corner
there are more positive faces
and less and less negative faces.

But the coolest thing is
I already know
I WIN!!!

My Inalienable Rights

I have the right to
the pursuit of happiness

I have the right to
take authority in and over my life

I have the right to love

I have the right to hurt

BUT I DON'T HAVE:

The right to
give in

The right to
give up

The right to
stop loving

Stop caring

Stop hoping

Out There

"Do you know where you're going to?"
"Do you like the things in life that are showing you?"
"Where are you going to, do you know?"

That was our class song in 1977.

I have placed my life in God's hand.
I can't tell you exactly where I'm going to,
but I do like the things in life that are showing me
where I'm going to.

God's road signs:
"Go to St. Louis"
"Go to Baton Rouge"
"Look to the hills from whence cometh your help"
"Press on"
"Lo I am with you always"
"Stay steady"
and
"This too, shall pass"

Rest Time

My concept of rest times:

There is a time to rest and re-energize the body
There is a time of rest for rejuvenation
There is a time of rest from the battle
There is a time of rest for meditation and prayer
There is a time of rest to reflect and strategize
There is a time of rest to see and hear
There is a time of rest for weariness

Rest time is never for:

Idleness
Stewing
Plotting revenge
Rehearsing what wrongs have been done to us

Over or Under

I got over
Or did I
I thought I got over
So why do I feel so down under

The *TRUTH* is:
I got over with the word of God

I am not under
I have just been presented with new challenges to
overcome

I overcome by my faith and the word of my testimony
As I move from glory to glory

Revelation
(inspired by T.D. Jakes)

I just received a revelation
Of what my current battle is

The enemy is after my faith
But I am battling to hold on to it

If he can get my faith
Then he'll have my hope
And I'll become angry & bitter

Well guess what devil,
You're a liar!
Now I know what sword I need

Jesus prayed that Peter wouldn't lose his faith
That's my prayer & my determination

I have to stand on faith building scriptures
I have to know God is God
And He's faithful

Satan I won't succumb to your lies,
I'm coming at you with the word of God.
What you meant for evil is only going to work for my
good
Because I'm the daughter of the Most High.

I'm fulfilling a purpose!

Speak to My Heart Lord

I am often plagued with the desire to quit
Constantly being bombarded with thoughts
"this is too hard"
"you'll never be able to really do this"
"all you do is screw up"
And so many more

A fact I learned a long time ago
"winners never quit, and quitters never win"
I have allowed myself to be sidetracked before

NOT THIS TIME
THE DEVIL IS A LIE!!!!

SPEAK TO MY HEART LORD~~~~

Survivor

I am a survivor!

I come from a long line of survivors
A lineage of ancestors
Who persevered against all odds

Who lived
Though death stared them in the face

Who fought and died for the survival
And future of their seed

Oh, yes I am a survivor!
But there is so much more to life
Then just surviving.

Truth or Fact
(inspired by Donna Frank)

John 16:33 was illuminated to me.
My peace is in Jesus.

When faced with situations and decision-making
The first thing I need to consider is
"Where is my peace."

When making a decision
Is there peace with the decision?

This just reiterates to me
There is no need for depression
(something I have suffered with for years).
I am so thankful for being set free
and delivered from depression.

But here it is,
Right here in John 16:33!

The fact is
I'm going to have my problems.
They may even look or feel overwhelming.

But the truth is
Jesus has overcome the world.
So I am to be of good cheer.

The bottom-line is
I must choose
"Will I believe the facts (what I am faced with)
or will I believe the truth (the word of God)?"

Wrestling with God
(Inspired by T. D. Jakes)

Up here on Penuel

"I won't let go!"

"Tell me my name!"

Yea Though I Walk
Through the Valley of The Shadow of Death

I said "yes, Lord" and it all began.

I find myself
on a journey I never even dreamed of.
I find myself
traveling through hills and mountains.
Sometimes through valleys and desserts.

But I also enjoy
the beauty that surrounds me.
I enjoy
the rest when it comes.
I enjoy
the pressing through (even when it is difficult).

No matter where this journey may lead,
there is one thing
I take great comfort in,
And that is...
That my hope,
my trust,
my faith
my total being
is in God.

He directs me,
He encourages me,
He teaches me,
He corrects me,
He shelters me,
but most of all
HE LOVES ME!!!

HALLWAY
VI

Enter with caution

A Battle Within

Went to sleep early
Woke up hungry
And entangled in a ball of emotions

Bewildered, yet lucid

Feeling betrayed
But not really believing
I've actually been betrayed

Wanting to stay
But wanting to go

Hurt
But not understanding
Why the actions of others
Have afflicted me so

Missing folks
But needing to be isolated

Wanting to be angry
But about what
And why

Feeling love
But not feeling loved

Lost
Even though I know
I'm on course

Wondering
Can they really not see
Or
Do they somehow see
Something different than the obvious

Thinking and questioning
Should I be trusting my heart
Or trusting my mind

Expecting, but leery

Believing but unable to see
(and this doesn't feel like faith)

Cognizant, yet foggy

Excited
Though a feeling of dread
Loops overhead

Wishing I could make things disappear
But knowing it wouldn't help
Even if I could

It's like sometimes when
I'm driving a familiar path
I know I'm going in the right direction
Yet everything seems so unfamiliar
I must keep assuring myself with landmarks

The sounds of silence
Pound against the walls of my mind
On the verge of a
TOTAL EXPLOSION

Fighting the Spirit of Suicide

When the spirit of suicide beacons
It's not something that is easily ignored

Knowing that God is on the throne
is not always enough....
Knowing that suicide is a totally selfish act
is not always enough....
Knowing how much you are going to hurt the ones who
love you
is not always enough....

And you know why?
Because suicide is a spirit.
You can't fight a spirit with knowledge.
You can only fight a spirit with The Spirit.

Cry out "Lord help me!"
Plea the blood of Jesus
over your body, mind and soul.
Yes! There is power in the blood!

Speak the word of God
OUT LOUD!
Praise and Worship
OUT LOUD!

As you fight that spirit
With The Spirit

The spirit of suicide
Will have to flee!

Just Another Day

UGH!!!!!!!!!!!!!!!!!!!!!!!

Hate,
Anger,
Fear,
Frustration!!!

Winners never quit and quitters never win,
quitters never win and winners never quit,
Winners never....................................
and so on, and so on!

UGH!!!!!!!!!!!!!!!!!!!!!!!!!!!!

But still knowing and feeling assure
that God has got it all in control!

So is my glass

\~/

Haff empty or Haff full?

NOW I LAY ME DOWN TO SLEEP

Now I lay me down to sleep
I pray the Lord my soul to keep
If I should die before I wake
I pray the Lord my soul to take

Not wanting to live anymore
But not suicidal
If I don't wake up in the morning
I won't be mad

Really and truly
I just don't want to be here anymore.
I WANT to sleep again
I WANT the pain to leave my body
I WANT the numbness to go away

I don't want to continue to live behind this mask
It is tiring and draining, it's wearing me out
But then again, I don't want the world
To see the me that I have become

I cried out
But I was not heard
I felt they wanted me to shut-up
So I did

And thus, the mask

You say, "how are you?"
I say "fine."
Living the lie that makes
Everyone else feel comfortable

Now that I'm quiet
You say
"you seem to really be doing better now"

When in fact I am struggling
To make it through yet another day

Wishing that I was no longer here
But I'm stuck here

Here
is trying to defeat me
Destroy me
Yes, even kill me.

No one really knows I'm here
So at the end of this day
I pray once more
Now I lay me down to sleep..........

S.O.S.

Here I am sitting in the bathroom
Lord, what is going on?

HELP ME PLEASE!!!!!
S.O.S!!!!!!
JESUS, JESUS, JESUS!!!!!

I want to leave
I want me out of the picture
I want to understand what I am feeling
HELP!!!!!

I want to stay in this bathroom
And never come out!

Life won't stop......not even for a minute

Special Days

Humanless Days
a day where there is no interaction or communication
with anyone;
not in person, not by phone, not by any of today's
technology
(text, email, etc.)
however, I do like to observe people if I can;
through an open window, from a car, etc.
and T.V. is okay
when I no longer want to think anymore

Alone in A Crowd Days
this is a day when I go to a crowded place to be alone;
a restaurant, movie, etc.
on these days I don't mind, in fact I enjoy
having a brief interaction with a complete stranger

Social Days
kickin' it with friends and/or family;
playing games, going out to eat, etc.

I have a great need and desire
to be alone a lot of the time.
The normal relationships of life
have a tendency to stress me out.

Hermit - a person who has withdrawn from society and
lives a solitary existence; a recluse

Doesn't sound bad to me.

Am I a nut?
I don't think so!

Suicide Trilogy

PART 1
A prayer of freedom

Dear Heavenly Father,
I come to you with thanksgiving in my heart
and praise on my lips.
Lord I thank you for deliverance
from the spirits of suicide and depression.
Lord I pray for the person who is now reading this.
I come against the spirits of suicide and depression
and I command them to leave
and stop tormenting this person,
in the Name of Jesus.

Lord I pray you will touch this person
and set him/her free.
I pray soul salvation
and your destiny for his/her life.
Lord reassure this person
that you will never leave him/her or forsake him/her.
And that there is nothing too hard to overcome
with the Lord at their side.
Lord make a way of escape,
open the eyes of the person who is now reading this
and show him/her to the way out of this particular
moment.

Let there be a peace within the spirit
of the person who is now reading this.
Let it be known no matter how dark the night,
joy comes in the morning.
This I pray
in the precious Name of Jesus Christ,
so let it be!!!!!

PART 2
The Spirit of Suicide is a Lie

I don't know
who you are
that may be
reading this today,
but I do know
that this prayer is for you!

I have dealt with the spirits of suicide and depression
since the age of 11.
I have attempted suicide on several occasions.

One thing I know is
that suicide is not necessarily wanting to be dead.
It's wanting to escape and be set free
from the situations and feelings
that seem to be overwhelming
and just too hard to deal with.

It's wanting a way out
because we cannot bear this pain for another minute.
We can't see that the pain will ever end.
We just can't continue to live with such intense pain
and this endless hopelessness.

Jesus can ease that pain
and even stop the pain.
One of the problems is
we just can't see the light at the end of the tunnel.
We have no hope.

Well Jesus Christ became and is my HOPE!
My life is in Jesus,
my hope is in Jesus,
my total being is in Jesus.

I can't even tell you the many times
He has brought me through.

When all my strength and hope was gone,
when there was nothing left in me to go on,
I then turned to Jesus.

Truly,
He has never left me or forsook me.
He's bought me through time and time again.
I have been hopeless, penniless, sick, confused,
and completely and utterly heartbroken.
Not able to see pass the pain.
But nevertheless
He's always been there for me.
Carrying me at times when I could not carry myself.

Even when I didn't really believe there was a God,
all I could do was HOPE there was a God,
He was there for me even then!!!!
THERE IS HOPE,
THERE IS A WAY OUT,
AND THERE IS DEFINITELY LIGHT
AT THE END OF THAT DARK TUNNEL.

I truly love and care for you
just because I know how it feels,
(or should I say because I know how bad it feels).
But Jesus loves you more than I ever could.
So today I proclaim in the name of Jesus
that you
'SHALL LIVE AND NOT DIE'

I hate the spirit of suicide
and I hate the spirit of depression,

so, I will continue to come against them
in the mighty Name of Jesus
each and every time
they raise their ugly little heads

I have been set free, appointed and anointed,
as long as there is breath in my body
I will continue to come against those debilitating spirits.

One last thing
don't ever let your feelings of suicide (really the spirits)
make you feel ashamed, weak, hopeless and less than.

Realize you are a child of the Most High God.
All you have to do is accept Jesus Christ into your life.

You should really know,
The mere fact that satan has attempted to attack you
like this
is because he is scared to death of you!
That is why he wants you dead.
Just the fact that you are still here means you have the
victory!

Believe me,
when you ask Jesus to help you
He will.
Things are not going to change overnight.
But Jesus will help you through
to the next second,
the next minute,
the next hour,
the next day, etc.
You too have been appointed,
and your destiny
has satan scared to death.

PART 3
PRAYER OF SALVATION

Dear Jesus,
I invite you into my life.
Please come in and be my Lord and Savior.

I believe you died upon the cross so that I could be set
free.
I turn my back on sin and invite you into my life.
I believe that **right this very minute** I have received
salvation
and that from this day forward
I am a child of the Most High God.

Lord I can't go on without Your help.

So today I surrender my all to you,
please have Your way in my life.
Teach me and show me how to continue to live,
bring me to my appointed destiny.
I pray this prayer in Jesus name
and I thank you for salvation.

Amen

That Scream

Have you ever heard
That Scream

That Scream
of anguish

That Scream
of total unbelief

That Scream
from so deep inside

That Scream
that knocks you to your knees

I remember the 1st time I heard
That Scream
October 28, 1993 (my birthday)
It came from my mother's room
She had just been told my aunt died

Next time I heard
That Scream
It came from me
When I was told my nephew was dead

I will never forget
That Scream

Have you ever heard
That Scream

The Beckoning

I close my eyes
And I see that noose again

Calling me
Beckoning me...........

.........I SHALL NOT DIE
BUT LIVE
AND DECLARE
THE WORKS OF THE LORD!

PSALM 118

Tunnel Vision

I am not a depression expert,
but I consider myself pretty well versed in depression.
My credentials are not academic
but from having lived through it.

When people are depressed
they are stuck in a very dark tunnel
and cannot see the light at the end of the tunnel.

Unfortunately, it's not just a straight tunnel;
it's a tunnel with all kinds of crazy turns
that lead to caves and pitfalls.

Unless you have made your way through the
tunnel
it is very difficult finding your way out.
Some of the pitfalls seem almost impossible
to climb up out of;
and when you do climb up
you are left still trying to
navigate your way through the dark tunnel.

While in the tunnel you have a couple of choices;
you can give up
and succumb to the darkness (*suicide*)

Or you can light a candle
and try to navigate your way
through the darkness.
But it gets very frustrating
because the candle doesn't stay lit;
you must keep lighting it
and hope you don't run out of matches
(*up today, down tomorrow*)

124

Or you can set up house in one of the caves
and try to pretend you are not really lost in a
tunnel
(*drugs, alcohol, etc.*)

Or you can cry out for help

I've done all the above!!!!!!!!!!!!!!

When I was in the tunnel
I didn't realize
there was a rescue party out there.

Once I started to cry out
They were able to follow my voice
and find me and lead me out.

But because I had been in the tunnel for so long
full of fear, despair and mistrust,
I fought the first rescue attempts.

But then one day
I heard a loving voice saying
"I am sending you help, please accept it".
(*Psalm 107*)

WHAT IS THIS THING CALLED LOVE

"I love you"
"Let's have sex"
"No"
Love vanishes

"I love you"
In the heat of the moment
Then when the moment passes
Love vanishes

"I love you"
"I can talk to you"
"You understand me"
Translation:
I like that I can dump on you

But when I am going through
When I am weak
When I don't have anything to give
Or the energy to listen
Or tend to your needs
Love vanishes

"I love you"
"You are my sister"
"I love you with the love of Christ"
I quit coming to church
Love vanishes

I'm sorry I can't accept that kind of love
Love remains
Love is.....

Love is not something you fall in and out of
Love does not end or change with circumstances
Love is not something you do out of obligation

To me
Love is unconditional
Love is everlasting
Love is never "done"

You don't have to love me back
in order for me to love you!!!

I'm gonna love you
Whether or not you love me

I'm gonna love you
Even when you don't have time for me

I'm gonna love you
When you don't do what I want you to do

I'm gonna love you
Especially when I see you going the wrong way

I'm gonna love you
I see the wall
but I don't care

I'm gonna love you
Even though you just hurt my feelings

I'm gonna love you
When you are no longer here

I'm gonna love you
Through anger, disappointment, harsh words........

Of course
I'm going to love you
Through the good times
That's easy
But love is not easy

For God so loved the world
That he gave His only begotten son

Greater love hath no man than this
that a man lay down his life for his friends

Please don't say you love me
Unless you really do

Please don't expect me to say I love you
Unless I really do

WHERE IS YOUR PEACE
(inspired by Alliece Cole)

There she stood
This red-haired woman asking
"where is your peace?"

A question that was so profound to me
I applied it to my life
When making decisions small or large
I would ask myself where is your peace?
Do I stay or go?
Where do I go?
How do I go?
Yea or nay?
Now or later?
With whom?

But all of a sudden
Peace has totally eluded me
I have no idea where my peace is
How did it just disappear?

You Hurt Me

I spent a lifetime
Building walls to protect myself

But I allowed you to penetrate those walls
And you hurt me........

Sometimes I feel
I want to hate you
Or hurt you worse
Because you hurt me......

But really and truly
I just want you
To make the hurt go away
But because you can't

I will just allow the walls to be repaired
And consider this
A lesson learned.

HALLWAY

VII

It's in the blood

Ache
(written by Akilah Nayo Oliver)

at my purest once,

in response to

what do you want

I said

I said

I just want to know God

Becoming Me
(written by Myesha Oliver)

Coming into my own
Discovering what I like
And what I don't

Seeing what I want to be
And making necessary changes
Seeing who I am now
Not who I used to be

Understanding that feelings and emotions are a part of
me
Realizing that my sensitivity doesn't make Me weak
And that my mean tendencies don't make Me a "B"

And although I'm not like most
I'm not the only one
Who thinks and feels and is just as guarded as I once
was

See I'm becoming Me
The beautifully unique being that God has called Me to
be
I'm not saying I'm the greatest or the best by any means

But I am saying
that I have recognized room for improvement on certain
things
Not really changing the core of what makes Me Me
Just improving the essences of what makes Me Me

See I'm becoming Me
I'm not all the way there yet
but loving the journey every minute of it
I love what I'm becoming
From the girl to the young woman to the woman to the
lady.

Because I'm becoming.....Me

Mean, bitter, sarcastic, guarded, self centered and cold
are all words that can be
used to describe my flaws
but caring giving dependable, honest, virtuous
trustworthy, and admirable are all words used to
describe my qualities
All of these words from my flaws to my qualities make
Me who I am
And I'm learning there's a time and place for all of them

It's harder than I thought to become a lady
Without being placed in a box of what a lady should be
The expectations put on me I know I can achieve
'Cause all of them shows Me what I can be
I'm becoming Me

Joy, hurt, pain, and excellence
Love, trust, honor, and self assurance
They're all a part of Me

And don't get it twisted
I'm not the only one with doubt and hesitation about my
womanhood
But that's a part of becoming Me

The strong beautiful and courageous woman I long to
be
I'm becoming Myesha, MyMy, Esha, Heaven Oliver
Whatever you choose to call Me

And it feels good to finally accept Me for Me
I'm becoming......Me

Crazy
(written by Myesha Oliver)

I'm crazy cause I work all day and night without sleep
Doing so much I have to be reminded to even eat

But the business I wanna be in
I gotta come in excellence
Aside from all the studying
I gotta come with experience
Gotta have the right state of mind

Be humble and confident at the same time
From the way that I dress
To the way that I sing
It all has to be correct

Gotta keep my swagger high
Even when I'm a mess and just chillin out
Gotta make sure my mess looks like you going out
Cause I'm taking it to the top and leaving others behind

When you start fading out I'll be multiplying
In all that I do and all that I say
Making sure you stay reciting my name day after day
So, you say I'm crazy and that's ok
Cause it seems to Me the crazy ones are here to stay!!

Dear Music
(written by Myesha Oliver)

Dear music,
I used to be a fan of you
And all the possibilities you brought
I used to love all the things you stood for
And all the difference you made
Music, my love for you is ocean deep
And as wide as the galaxy
But my hatred for you increases
I hate what they made you
I hate how you conformed
But I love you more than life itself
That won't ever change
Music, don't you realize your power
Don't you see your influence
Music the universal language
The universal poison
Music you put a move on my heart
And I hate that I love you
I'm dangerously crazy in love with you
I even love the way you lie
Music, you were my redemption
And you're now my destruction
Empowering and manipulating
Dangerous combination
Music, you been so much to me
Now let me be the same for you
Dear music, I am here to save you

Ode to My Aunt Akilah
(written by Marqueta Oliver)

Play me some music
Make me some tea
A bowl of coffee ice cream please
Sara Lee pound cake too
Read to me
Laugh with me
Share with me a secret
Stay up late with me and giggle
Talk on the phone like girlfriends
Take me to the beach
Take me to the park
Take me to the museum
Take me to the rose garden
Talk to me...
I'm listening

Poem for Mother
December 1981
(written by Donna (Akilah) Oliver)

in myself so much
i see her there
i, who always loved her but rarely understood
thought she was to be treated
something like a precious rare object
instead of like
the precious rare living strength she is
objects of course can be ignored

in myself so much
i feel her there
sometimes i thought that all i had
was mine created and owned
and if that is so then
she gave me all which allowed me to create
we are intricately bound

i understand now
why i hurt when her spirits flounder
never having been unleashed from their chains
never having been explored in their true captivity
she was busy
raising four kids

complete me mamma
i want to see you soar

Resolution 2010
(written by Marqueta Oliver)

Why does my ambition make you feel so uncomfortable?
My success and my drive,
Really seem to make you miserable

I've caused you no malice, no hurt and no harm
Are you really that consumed with my style and my
charm?

I'm just doin' me
Trying to live my life to the fullest
And you're choosing to be a pawn
In my life's game of chess

C'mon now, do we really have to do this?
Try to make each other fall?
Turns out we can actually both have it all...
The world really isn't that small!

You don't have to play a supporting role in this life
Where I'm boss
You can choose to have your own starring role
And allow our paths just to cross...

We really don't need to be going through this mess
Distressed with unnecessary crap!
You're like an evil prophet
Declaring how special I am

Your hatred,
Spreads my popularity
Which pushes me more to be all that I am!!!!!
It must be frustrating
seeing your foul intent help guide my path

The Epitome of Grown and Sexy
(written by Marqueta Oliver)

Please don't come at me left
Mr. All Swagged Out

In order to step to me right
You must find out what I'm all about

Don't judge my head held high
As me thinking I'm too good

I just know my value
So you must talk to me the way a man should

Before you start trying to think about
How to make me moan

I challenge you to look into my eyes
And tell me
Can you see my soul?

The attire I wear
is meant for you to stop and stare

It's a reflection of my pride
From my shoes to my hair

The fact that I have my own
Shows that I'm reaping what I've sown

So, I'm not entertained by games
Cause......Baby I'm quite too grown

No, I'm not a tease
I'm just a lady
and I'm not easy

143

But I know that you'll be pleased
When I turn on my sexy

For me, grown and sexy is
A party or an event...

It's the way that I walk,
The essence of my style....

It's my very scent!

Warm Hearted

(Written by Andrae (A.J.) Blissett, Jr age 8)

Roses are Red
Violets are blue
These are the flowers
That remind me of you!

You are loving, kind and beautiful
You are the one that is a joy
To God and the earth

But sometimes you can be mean
But we know in our hearts
You still love us

And your name is Melvaline Oliver
And you are warm hearted

Dear Reader,

Welcome to my world.

This book was birthed at a very difficult time in my life. In 2009 I found myself in Indianapolis, Indiana with my mom, who had been diagnosed with stage 5 lung cancer. During the late-night hours, I needed to do something with my mind, one night as I was praying the Lord told me to write. I was with my mom for 3 months before she went on home. I found myself experiencing feelings I still can't describe.

I continued to write my book after I returned to Baton Rouge, Louisiana. In the latter part of 2010 I shared with my sister Akilah about my book. My sister is an internationally published author. She was quite an encouragement to me as I worked on the book. She said she would help be publish my book. I had my sights set on getting the book published in 2011, and then the unthinkable happened! My sister was found dead in her New York apartment in February 2011. She never got a chance to read the book. The irony of the whole thing is that I had written the acknowledgement that same night in Indianapolis when the Lord told me to write the book, this was before my sister ever knew about the book.

I was still struggling with my mom's death, mostly just missing her not being here. My sister's death hit me harder than I could ever have expected. I spent the entire year on a downward spiral (I really didn't realize how much I was spiraling).

I did absolutely nothing with my book (though I did read one of the poems at my sister's funeral). The death of my mom and sister left me with such intense pain and emptiness I could not imagine that I would ever truly be happy in life again.

I begin to cut off all ties; let church slip completely out of my life. Though I continued to hold on to God by a thread, it all came to a head one night. After all these years of deliverance I found myself once again in 2012 trying to commit suicide. Thank God I failed. The realization of what I had attempted to do made me realize how far I had fallen.

One night I was texting back and forth with a friend (who knew of my suicide attempt), she encouraged me to make sure I continue to go to church as though my life depended upon it. At that point and time, I knew that my life did, in fact, depend on me renewing my relationship with God, I immediately repented!

Yet I was still being beckoned daily by suicidal thoughts. Each morning having to remind myself "You will live and not die to declare the works of the Lord". Reminding myself of my 2 beautiful daughters who would probably be devastated by my untimely death. It wasn't that I really wanted to die, I was just having such a hard and painful time living.

I decided to share with my friend via text that though I was pretty sure I was no longer suicidal; I was still struggling to live. That is when the Holy Spirit spoke to me "read your book."

I thought to myself I no longer had a desire to publish that book or do anything else with it. I began to prepare to go to bed. Again, I heard "read your book", immediately I pulled up my book on my laptop and looked through the table of contents. And there it was "Suicide Trilogy", I scrolled down to it, I started reading it *Lord, I pray for the person who is now reading this* (wait a minute I am the person reading this!) and then I started praying it.

It was the Holy Spirit who inspired me to write this book and it was the Holy Spirit who was using the same inspired book to encourage me.
I realized it didn't matter whether I wanted to publish this book; I had to publish this book because it needed to be read. God had a plan for this book, and it wasn't just for me!

Then came my trip to St. Louis to face yet another death, my cousin Stanley. In his hospital room praying, worshipping and praising God; I felt so unworthy. I felt like a perpetrator, I had fallen so far away from God. The family prayed, sang and ushered Stanley into death. Once again, I texted my friend and told her my cousin had passed. She texted back her condolences and warned me to be careful not to fall into "eternal grief". What a revelation! In the last 2 years I had spiraled into "eternal grief" (a very dark place). As I prayed for deliverance, God delivered me, brushed me off, placed my feet on solid ground and with love He said "You are who I say you are" So I returned to work on my book again and with the guidance of the Holy Spirit this book has now been published.

150

"He who started a good work in me, has been faithful to complete it"
February 2020

I pray this book is a blessing to all those who read it. I don't care what it looks like or what it is, allow God to show you the answer!

Order INFO

	Price $19.75 per book	

Please allow 7 – 10 days for shipment

Orders can be placed via

    1) PayPal – paypal.me/marcidy
    2) marciaissetfree@aol.com
    3) Amazon.com

Marcia's vision is to open a maternity home for unwed mothers. She has a heart for young women, to build their esteem and help them realize their value and purpose.

THANK YOU

Made in the USA
Monee, IL
10 July 2020

36240709R00090